Somewhere Between Rose and Black

Claire Walker

V.

Published in the United Kingdom in 2017

by V. Press,

10 Vernon Grove,

Droitwich,

Worcestershire,

WR9 9LQ.

ISBN: 978-0-9935508-7-4

Acknowledgements

Acknowledgements are due to the editors of the following publications in which some of the poems, or versions of, have appeared: Algebra of Owls, Amaryllis, Clear Poetry, The Poetry Shed.

Thanks to Anne Milton, Liz Parkes, Ian Glass and the Worcestershire Poetry Society Stanza for their feedback, support and encouragement with these poems. Thank you to Ruth Stacey for her faith in this pamphlet, and for her beautiful artwork, and to Sarah Leavesley for her invaluable support and advice.

Thank you to Rich and Anna for always being there.

V.

For my mum and Betty, and for Mollie -

whose diary inspired these poems.

V.

Contents

V.

Moving

The sky hangs a different way. Light slants,
flashes as the van rolls along dirt tracks to the door.
A key in the broken lock. His hand finds mine,
our fingers knot as we cross the threshold.

While we stack boxes on bare boards,
that sky is everywhere –
it peers into windows, down through
a shredded roof. The clouds drift on

and on, make judgements as they pass.
Our shell of sticks blown down
by night creatures, waiting for us
to puzzle walls back together.

I stand in the doorway,
watch the sun arch swollen frames.
It binds all things. Skeleton house,
this sky will know if I fail to build a home.

Merging with the Forest

My first glimpse is through an open window.
An almost-thing darts across:
hint in a field. I notice graceful legs
that pause, briefly, a nose bends
to nuzzle shoots in the grass.
The slope of his neck tells me this is his table.
Rising again, his antlers merge with the forest,
those endless trees that tangle to sky;
the border of this world.

Planting has Begun

I've never known a garden so big.
The breadth of the house, it flows
around corners, out of eye-line.

I untangle brambles, bring the ground
back into view. Hope calms my feet
beside clusters of earth.

Birds hop in time to my thoughts,
sow ideas of how to tame wildness.
They settle close and sing.

I rake ground over to even lines;
plant daffodils for fresh beginnings,
push gnarled bulbs into giving soil.

Building Materials

If I lie on the kitchen floor,
my back shrinking from cold quarry stone,
I can see the night's purple sky.

The roof isn't yet fixed. He tries,
works hard against the weather,
but this is only one of many jobs.

His arms, that used to reach for me,
are always full of bricks,
his mouth full of clay.

I watch the moon through fallen tiles.
Tomorrow we must steady them
against the threat of rain.

Presence

I give up watching for antlers
through the dark. Lying awake,
I know their presence:
the gnaw of teeth against the night.

I've begun to identify with them. Come dawn,
I slip my feet inside the print of hooves,
touch their bite marks with my fingers,
taste early shoots on my tongue.

I plant for deer now;
sow peas to feed hungry nights,
realise nothing can grow to full height,
accept the elegant destruction.

Feeding the Jays

I hung up the sheep's breastbone –
my bird table offering for the year's infant months.
I could sense fear when they first flew by,
cautious twitching heads as they weighed their safety.

Persuaded, their ravenous beaks set to work,
stopping only occasionally to flit, amused,
around the rack. Such appetite,
despite being only the size of my hand.

This was not a selfless gift. Days lighten
when I see those green wings fly in,
black heads bobbing for the fat they hunger for.
Winter has been sparse, we're all desperate to be full.

Young Robins

I thought of them as children.
Early morning, their insistent beaks
would tap the window for food,
perched on their window-sill cot.
I learned their tastes, fed sunflower
seeds from my palm.
I watched fluffed feathers grow smooth
against growing bodies.
In the skies that came,
they chose the garden's touch
instead of mine. Paired,
they grew shy, sought the hedge-lining,
jumped the border and flew to their own nest,
away from human eyes.

Limewashing the Cottage

To stop weathering, the resolute damp,
there was no choice
but pull down the honeysuckle.

This striking plant had taken to the soil,
rooted there, climbed brick to brick
until it claimed the south side of the house.

Yellow petals uncurled,
pink tips stretched to air, leaving
their closed-bud cocoon for a taste of June.

A sparrow had built her nest inside,
used twined ladders to tether her home.
I must try to salvage it for the young;

try to tie the honeysuckle back in place
now the limewash has dried hard.
The things we do to protect our walls.

Two Birds Join Me for Coffee

They must have heard the kettle's whistle,
a sound, as if from their own beaks,
to signal a rest for elevenses.

When I sat down at the kitchen table,
those sparrows chirped their conversation
as if I'd set a cup and saucer for them both.

As they cased the rafters for a nesting site,
I could believe the room was airy,
that I too had feathers and a beak full of verse.

At the door I hoped their notes were promises.
As they flew higher than the roof,
I felt the pinch of my flightless wings.

The Only Good Day

Today, the river is high.
As I walk by its side,
I feel the wet-mud pull,
wonder how far I'd sink
if I dared stop moving.
Water lies stagnant in the field.

I have watched every storm:
the thunder throwing
greenhouse glass across the garden;
the wind culling nests from trees.

More storms than days this month,
the only relief was the tenth:
the sun was listless, weak
after its water-logged battle,
but there was definitely warmth
on my face. I wonder if it's enough?
Today, the river is high.

Marriage

I slip
between journal pages.

Words are no longer purely fact –
I see the metaphor in storm-talk,
my repetitions of fallen nests, failing plants,
trying to decide if earth is working
for or against me.

He is a good man
but I am cold in this half-built home,
its damp, heartless hearth.
I want the lightning-cracks
that laughter ignites between bodies,

the lit-fire eyes of compatible minds.
What is the point of reconstruction?
These walls remain uneven,
draughts still shudder past the door.
I leave my walking boots facing the forest,

wonder
if he can read meanings.

Deer in a Storm

I watch clouds pit themselves
against each other. Rolls of thunder
are out-matched by rain's persistence.

The deer are hardier than me:
I shudder at the slightest breeze,
feel this shell rattle in the wind.

They weather storms like old oaks.
The branches of their antlers carve
through battling skies.

Winds blow the scent of food towards them.
Their noses compass a way to the garden,
their hooves never buckle.

The man in the farmhouse

holds me with his words
when he comes to check
we're still standing after the storm.
The fruit trees remain unbowed,
but he notices our stolen crops, laughs boldly
that deer are more destructive than any weather.
This neighbour understands their dark beauty.

Later, we dine with his family,
warm within thick walls.
So much heat is kept inside.
He plays cards with my husband
while I talk to his wife,
stack flowered china in the rack.

The man in the farmhouse
holds me with his eyes
when we say goodbye on the dark front step.
An owl hoots in a distance I shrug off.
Bats loop my house and his.

Lone Stag

I see him, as I tie the beans to bamboo,
secure our supplies against twilight.
Lone stag, antlers open to fading sky,
only the low, splintered fence between us.

I move slowly – intrigued, sliding my feet – and there we are,
faces close, his nose jutting over the divide.
He smells clover, but his eyes rest on me,
gentle brown irises considering his provider.

My hand finds his coat, soft against muscle,
the mottled baby-back long outgrown.
Reaching his neck, I touch cool antlers,
feel the even planes that fork to weather.

I struggle to breathe for the magic of him,
this garden enemy – the reason our plates are empty,
our beds full of holes. I am frightened,
but don't want him to vanish.

Trespass

In theory, I'm trespassing. I climb
the gate, its weight easily holds my bones,
the cotton dress of my skin.
I cannot resist the height of this field,
the ears of wheat up to my waist.

Here, I will find him,
walking his dog in early evening,
low sun slung on his back,
as he picks across the path
that feet and paws have made.

He doesn't expect me,
in between rows of crop.
His dog gauges my scent,
rubs a wet nose across my fingers,
wants me to stroke his coat.

We talk of light things,
the warmth of the hour;
the dog bounds, chases sticks we throw.
In this field, we're submerged in growth.
He doesn't tell me to leave.

Silhouettes

I shut out the dusk,
light a candle in every room.
The flare ignites shadow puppets
across the walls – dog, deer, a man.
I start a fire, add my own silhouette.
We dance around each other,
I stroke their dark heads,
ask the stag for his thoughts.

I could forget the roof, wrapped
in this comfortable place between
shadow and flame. Yet it leaks –
a single drop snuffs out pictured shapes.
It leaves me stilled, faded into wall.
The man shrinks, I hear his dog growl.

Cultivation

In spare hours I pull unwanted life from soil.
My hands easily uproot weeds –
some fight back, prick my fingers,
cling to the plot they have claimed.
As I work, I hear birds overhead.
I think how they sing softer than humans;
I think it as I rid beds of life I do not like.

Firing the Gun

In his fury, he strides to the farmhouse,
wishing for a gun in his hands.

I colour at the thought, burn
between loss and enchantment.
The gnawing is relentless, but
their antlers have cast a spell
I don't want to break.

I dread his shot, the still
carcass reddening the earth.
I imagine him wearing the pelt,
parading fallen magnificence
on his shoulders.

My mouthed warning goes unheard
through closed windows.
He takes aim while the stag bends
his slow neck to sweet ground.
I jolt at the firing, bunch
my eyelids in fear,

open them to fleeing hooves,
the trigger-pull out of range.

Pattern

I slip on the frozen step.
A lost footing and ice flaws me,
leaves me an outsider at the front door.

Suddenly he is there, arm guiding me,
I'm a snowflake at his touch.
Cold crystal, ready to thaw.

I imagine only he can read
the complex pattern of me, my shape
curved onto his blue iris.

Spirals and Corners

In this hallway – where no draughts
leave windows to shake in unpainted frames,
where photos of children spilled from the sea
stand smiling on a hand-carved table –
my eyes follow the sweep of staircase.

This is homemade space and light. Each brick
laid level, each wall coloured by his warm hands,
and those stairs curve like the spiral has no end.

I turn to face him, white stag of possibility.
He brushes his fingers across my face,
the swirl of his thumbprint holds on the apple of my cheek.

This is when I become aware of corners.
Hard angles of no escape,
a lack of places to hide.
I notice the gun, locked in its cabinet,
remember that my husband fired it last.

Captive Bird

He hands it over, this newspaper-wrapped
find he presents to me. I shed the layer of print,
his hopeful eyes on my hands
in these early hours.

I didn't expect something so pretty.
The porcelain smooth in my cupped hands,
lid balanced on top of the pot.
I recognise how fragile it feels.

The image is *Captive Bird.*
Blue handpainted mysteries
caught mid-swoop under the glaze.
A willow bows, prussian-dark, over water.

Here is where the day unfreezes.
This pot, ready to steep
to an octagon of warmth
on the worktop,

spout turned to the window,
facing the rising sun.
I scoop dusky leaves onto a teaspoon,
half expecting a canary to fly free.

No Damsons or Plums

i

When the frosts came, they came late.
Out of step with the season,
plants - caught off guard - crinkled away from light.

The lilacs were killed in bud,
the crisp air sending sharp stabs
to halt their petal hearts.

No damsons or plums to come
this year - the chill has left no autumn fruit
proving on feathered branches.

ii

Perhaps I can do without
their bruise of colour;
the stone when my teeth reach their core.

The weather has not spiked the summer fruits.
I still have August to come - its redcurrant tang;
the strawberry juice for my tongue, which will speak of life.

Apple Picking

Finally, something works.
The tree heaves beneath the weight -
that first flood of fruit; we pick,
store, rejoice.

Windfall offers enough to deer;
the branches remain full for us.
Green, blushing red in my hands -
life dressed in September colours.

Too sharp to eat raw,
they soften at golden sugar, simmered flames.
Flour and butter crumble through my fingers,
ready to blanket the sweetness.

Much is stored away. Jars, bottles,
anything that holds.
The whole ones nestle together, stalks entwined
in the pantry's sleeping dark.

We cannot contain it all.
Hot inside our thawing mouths, we smile
for each other, for the turning of earth.
We eat the evening, spoon by spoon.

White Christmas

The sky lightened yesterday evening.
I sensed change, scrabbled at the window
to pull dark curtains aside.
A soft and steady fall.
The silence of white landing on grass
smoothed the chaos of the day.

There is something in snow I need
to feel for myself. Outside,
my bare feet squirm on cold slabs
but my hands upturn, ask for more.
It is my childhood falling,
sparkling, to earth.

On Christmas Day we celebrate
the weather's gifts and faults;
toast the cottage's fixed roof.
New Year will dress unfinished rooms.
We settle, limewash merging
with this crisp, giving sky.

Somewhere Between Rose and Black

This evening I sit on the river bank,
sun low in the sky, wrapping my back.

I think of water, how it cares nothing
for deeds, good or bad. Whoever's chest
your head rests on, it will still smooth
prickles from your hair;
still swirl the softness of your body,
won't coil away in reproach.

I sit, the light drops somewhere
between rose and black.
I slip my feet inside the shallows -
know they would graze on the pebbled floor,
but the dusk-cooled water strokes them clean.

Claire Walker is a poet based in Worcestershire. Her work has been published in magazines and on websites including The Interpreter's House, Prole, Ink Sweat and Tears, And Other Poems, The Poetry Shed, Obsessed with Pipework and Clear Poetry, and in anthologies such as *The Chronicles of Eve* (Paper Swans Press) and *Crystal Voices* (Crystal Clear Creators). She is a Poetry Reader for Three Drops Press, and Co-Editor of Atrium poetry webzine. Her first pamphlet, *The Girl Who Grew Into a Crocodile*, is also published by V. Press.

V.